Sharpening Your Spiritual Tools

Sharpening Your Spiritual Tools

MELITON BARRON
&
VALENCIA TYSINGER

XULON PRESS

Xulon Press
2301 Lucien Way #415
Maitland, FL 32751
407.339.4217
www.xulonpress.com

© 2023 by Meliton Barron and Valencia Tysinger

All rights reserved solely by the author. The author guarantees all contents are original and do not infringe upon the legal rights of any other person or work. No part of this book may be reproduced in any form without the permission of the author.

Due to the changing nature of the Internet, if there are any web addresses, links, or URLs included in this manuscript, these may have been altered and may no longer be accessible. The views and opinions shared in this book belong solely to the author and do not necessarily reflect those of the publisher. The publisher therefore disclaims responsibility for the views or opinions expressed within the work.

Unless otherwise indicated, Scripture quotations taken from the King James Version (KJV)–*public domain.*

Paperback ISBN-13: 978-1-66287-484-0
Ebook ISBN-13: 978-1-66287-485-7

TABLE OF CONTENTS

Preface vii

Introduction........................... xi

Chapter 1 Tool # 1 – Word of God 1

Chapter 2 Tool # 2 – Prayer 9

Chapter 3 Tool # 3 – Praise and Worship 17

Chapter 4 Tool # 4 – Communion.......... 25

Chapter 5 Tool # 5 – Fasting.............. 35

Chapter 6 Tool # 6 – Hearing from God..... 47

Chapter 7 Tool # 7 – Spiritual Sight and Vision . 57

Chapter 8 Tool # 8 – Confess and Speak

                       God's Word 67

Prayer of Salvation 77

Afterword 79

Preface

During our work Bible study, the lesson of the day was "Sharpening Your Tools." The discussion of this lesson was interesting, enlightening, and powerful. It left me thinking how this message could be a blessing to others who heard it, and how it could help them have a closer walk with God. I was inspired to consider writing a book on "Sharpening Your *Spiritual* Tools." The Bible study was being taught by the co-author of this book, Valencia. We both agree that, now more than ever, God is collectively calling us as the people of God to walk in a greater level of spiritual growth and maturity, charging us to go higher in Him. We are called to enhance and intensify our spiritual connection with God, and allow His counsel to maneuver us through the pathway of life. He wants us to be a prepared people, so we won't be caught off-guard and misled by the Enemy and his tactics against us. For any opposition we face, God has given us a way out to gain victory.

God has equipped us with spiritual tools to help us effectively carry out our God-given assignments and to live godly, successfully, and flourish upon the earth in our spirit, soul, and body. For our weapons are of God (He is our defense), and are mighty in and through Him to cast down and destroy that which strives, fights, and contends against us. Using the armor and instruments of God helps provide the necessary protection in warfare against the Enemy. Instead of drawing back when we encounter adversities and challenges, knowing that we have power to overcome allows us to move forward in full assurance and confidence. In Scripture, the

Preface

words "weapon" and "armor" are more widely used than "tools," but nevertheless, they all are similar in that they add to and further improve our fruitfulness and authority as Christians.

It is our prayer that you journey with us through this book, and, as a result, you are enlightened and refined in the process. May this book be insightful in that it renews, uplifts, develops, and increases you further as God's chosen vessel. Also, we hope this reference of tools will be informative and a continual haven of support to reboot, shift, and catapult you to higher dimensions. Let change and transformation take flight in you!

We dedicate this book to God our Savior, in gratefulness and thankfulness to Him for the wonderful things He's done in, and through, our lives. To God be the glory! We thank our family for supporting us through this endeavor. Also, thank you to our Bible study sisters, who have encouraged us over the years.

Introduction

Do you desire to go higher in the Lord? Do you yearn for a more intimate walk with the Father? Well, God is calling us to a deeper and closer relationship with Him. His desire is that we walk in the purpose, destiny, and will of God. He has called us out of the kingdom of darkness, sin, and wickedness to be led by His kingdom of light and life. When we align ourselves and connect with the Holy Spirit of God, allowing Him to guide and instruct us, we benefit from the wisdom, understanding, and revelation of God's Word, and understand how it applies to our lives. God intends for us to live victorious lives full of His glory and power. Our time spent with the Lord is not wasted, so we should take advantage of being in constant and continual fellowship with Him because what we gain as a result is immeasurable.

To assist us in our Christian walk, God provided us with tools necessary to activate, maintain, and accomplish our responsibilities and duties, as we seek to do what His Word commands, and increase our understanding of His purpose and will for our lives as we advance in the kingdom of God. These tools may also be referred to as "instruments," "equipment," "weapons," (2 Cor. 10:4), or "armor," (Eph. 6:11). "Tools" are defined as "a device used to help carry out a particular function or task." Tools can make a task simpler and easier. They can also be used to change or shape the surrounding environment. In our development of walking as mature Christians, we should be focused and alert, as in 1 Peter 5:8, using our (spiritual) tools to help us win and conquer in the process, because the more we use

Introduction

them, the more prepared we are to face life's challenges.

There are times when it becomes necessary to sharpen the tools to better reflect the results we strive to achieve in hopes of being purged, enriched, and perfected in the process. The term "sharpen" means "to make better, improve, polish, and fine tune." It helps alleviate dullness of the current condition. Staying *sharp* allows us to remain ready and focused for God's use. We also need to remain sharp to cut through the Enemy's tactics and pitfalls laid out for us. The process can always be adjusted when necessary, redirecting our course for a greater outcome. There is always room for a more enhanced and cultivated you, especially when God is leading the improvement crew.

This book outlines and captures some of the various tools we have been given. They can be used in conjunction with what you may already be using. The book references supporting scriptures as to *why*

Sharpening Your Spiritual Tools

and *how*, in relation to each tool and then summarizes the tool. Also, it initiates self-reflection and examination through the application questions raised in each chapter, alongside a list of helpful "tool tips." It is our hope that you take notice of each tool and utilize them to give attention to any individual area that can be improved upon, and take the necessary steps to do so. We aspire for this book to be useful for individuals and Bible study groups alike; that, through your studying, learning, and meditating, you grow increasingly and exponentially. May you experience and encounter the Spirit of God in a magnificent way!

CHAPTER 1

TOOL #1 – WORD OF GOD

Why?

- This book of the law shall not depart out of thy mouth; but thou shalt meditate therein day and night, that thou mayest observe to do according to all that is written therein: for then thou shalt make thy way prosperous, and thou shalt have good success. (Josh. 1:8)

- All scripture is given by inspiration of God, and is profitable for doctrine, for reproof, for correction, for instruction in righteousness: That the man of God may be perfect, thoroughly furnished unto all good works. (2 Tim. 3:16-17)

- Thy word is a lamp unto my feet, and a light unto my path. (Ps. 119:105)

Tool #1 –Word of God

- The entrance of thy words giveth light; it giveth understanding unto the simple. (Ps. 119:130)

- My son, attend to my words; incline thine ear unto my sayings. Let them not depart from thine eyes; keep them in the midst of thine heart. For they are life unto those that find them, and health to all their flesh. (Prov. 4:20-22)

- So shall my word be that goeth forth out of my mouth: it shall not return unto me void, but it shall accomplish that which I please, and it shall prosper in the thing whereto I sent it. (Isa. 55:11)

How?

- Thy word have I hid in mine heart, that I might not sin against thee. (Ps. 119:11)

Sharpening Your Spiritual Tools

- So then, faith cometh by hearing, and hearing by the word of God. (Rom. 10:17)

- As newborn babes, desire the sincere milk of the word, that ye may grow thereby. (1 Pet. 2:2)

- But be ye doers of the word, and not hearers only, deceiving your own selves. (James 1:22)

- He sent his word, and healed them, and delivered them from their destructions. (Ps. 107:20)

- Study to shew thyself approved unto God, a workman that needeth not to be ashamed, rightly dividing the word of truth. (2 Tim. 2:15)

The Word of God, the Bible, is the most important book we will read. It was written to teach and instruct us in godly

Tool #1 –Word of God

and righteous living. It is part of our armor and spiritual equipment, through which we receive wisdom, knowledge, and understanding that can only come from God. As we study and meditate on the Word, it guides us to conform to the ways of God, and transforms us by renewing our minds. Also, we are able to find answers to situations and circumstances we face, to help encourage and uplift us. When we trust in the promises within God's Word, we walk in the victory that it provides.

Knowing what's in God's Word should not be taken lightly because we have to know what the Word says in order to obey it. It is to our own detriment when we don't regularly seek God through His Word. Seeing this is how we learn more about who He is and who we are in Him. As we gain insight, this helps us to connect the dots of what this life's journey is about. The Word is like hidden treasure: when searched out and answers are found, we are enlightened, we grow, and it becomes

Sharpening Your Spiritual Tools

a priceless jewel in our lives. It is our lifeline — a way of escape, a great source to help receive answers to prayer, and to keep us moving forward along the right path.

Furthermore, studying the Word will help us realize how significant it is that all Scripture is written by the inspiration and revelation of God. It is God-breathed, motivated, and influenced by the Spirit of God. His Word is not stale or antiquated, but alive, fresh, and powerful. His Word is true and will not return empty; it will accomplish what it set out to do. God watches over His Word to bring it to pass.

Tool Tips:

- Pray and ask God for understanding in His Word.

- Read and meditate on the Word daily.

- Read the Word in context.

- Use Bible tools that coincide with God's Word to gain further clarity of Scripture.

- Eliminate distractions when studying the Word of God.

- Journal what God speaks to you from His Word.

Application

What do you think is the importance of the ***Word of God***?

_____
_____
_____
_____
_____

Sharpening Your Spiritual Tools

How does this tool improve your daily walk with God?

_____
_____
_____
_____
_____

How can you share the Word of God with others?

_____
_____
_____
_____
_____

CHAPTER 2

Tool #2 – Prayer

Why?

- Let us therefore come boldly unto the throne of grace, that we may obtain mercy, and find grace to help in time of need. (Heb. 4:16)

- Likewise the Spirit also helpeth our infirmities: for we know not what we should pray for as we ought: but the Spirit itself maketh intercession for us with groanings which cannot be uttered. (Rom. 8:26)

- If my people, which are called by my name, shall humble themselves, and pray, and seek my face, and turn from their wicked ways; then will I hear from heaven, and will forgive their sin, and will heal their land. (2 Chron. 7:14)

- Be careful for nothing; but in every thing by prayer and supplication

Tool #2 – Prayer

with thanksgiving let your requests be made known unto God. (Phil. 4:6)

- Confess your faults one to another, and pray one for another, that ye may be healed. The effectual fervent prayer of a righteous man availeth much. (James 5:16)

- Call unto me, and I will answer thee, and shew thee great and mighty things, which thou knowest not. (Jer. 33:3)

How?

- Pray without ceasing. (1 Thess. 5:17)

- And this is the confidence that we have in him, that, if we ask any thing according to his will, he heareth us. (1 John 5:14)

Sharpening Your Spiritual Tools

- Therefore I say unto you, What things soever ye desire, when ye pray, believe that ye receive them, and ye shall have them. (Mark 11:24)

- And all things, whatsoever ye shall ask in prayer, believing, ye shall receive. (Matt. 21:22)

- Watch and pray, that ye enter not into temptation: the spirit indeed is willing, but the flesh is weak. (Matt. 26:41)

- Then shall ye call upon me, and ye shall go and pray unto me, and I will hearken unto you. (Jer. 29:12)

Through prayer, God has given us a way to boldly come to Him, whether by worship, adoration, and praise or by petition, supplication, and intercession. We have a direct line into the throne room of

Tool #2 – Prayer

God through Jesus Christ our Lord, and we have an audience of one with the Father. We can approach God confidently, in full assurance and trust, knowing as we agree with God's Word through prayer, His Word will accomplish what it was ordained to do. He's given us everything we need through knowledge of His Word. So, as we align our faith to believe God's Word, declaring it over us, it shall come to pass in our lives.

God allows us to communicate with Him instead of having to live a life of worry, stress, and fear. By prayer and thanksgiving to God, we can cast off all burdens and cares that we were never equipped to carry, and bask in the glory of being in fellowship and in the presence of our King. For as we commune with Him, we find strength, peace, and joy to quiet us, even when chaos and turmoil seem to be happening all around us. To be effective in prayer, get rid of any distractions that will hinder your focus on God. Exalt Him above all else, knowing we are to always pray and not lose heart.

Our prayer should not only involve us speaking to God, but also involve Him speaking to us. God is concerned about those things that concern us, and He wants to impart information to us. So, we should be listening for what God may want to reveal. As we listen, we become more discerning and are more sensitive to the Spirit of God. God also enjoys fellowship with His children. Our prayer time doesn't have to always be about us asking of the Father, but we can connect with Him, expressing our love and desire to be close to Him. Strive to pray daily and consistently; this increases our faith and belief in God, and causes spiritual growth within us.

Tool #2 – Prayer

Tool Tips:

- Pray in faith, believing and trusting God's Word.

- Pray promises found in God's Word based on Scripture.

- Pray daily and consistently.

- To limit distractions during your prayer time with God, use a quiet place, such as a prayer closet, prayer room, etc.

- Listen for God to speak to you during your time of prayer.

- Journal the thoughts you hear from God when you pray.

Application

Sharpening Your Spiritual Tools

What do you think is the importance of ***prayer***?

_____
_____
_____
_____
_____

How does this tool improve your daily walk with God?

_____
_____
_____
_____
_____

How does your prayer time with God help you grow?

_____
_____
_____
_____

CHAPTER 3

TOOL #3 – PRAISE AND WORSHIP

Why?

- God is a Spirit: and they that worship him must worship him in spirit and in truth. (John 4:24)

- I will praise thee; for I am fearfully and wonderfully made: marvelous are thy works; and that my soul knoweth right well. (Ps. 139:14)

- Because thy lovingkindness is better than life, my lips shall praise thee. (Ps. 63:3)

- This is the day which the Lord hath made; we will rejoice and be glad in it. (Ps. 118:24)

- Whoso offereth praise glorifieth me: and to him that ordereth his conversation aright will I shew the salvation of God. (Ps. 50:23)

Tool #3 – Praise and Worship

- O give thanks unto the Lord; for he is good: for his mercy endureth forever. (Ps. 136:1)

- Praise ye the Lord: for it is good to sing praises unto our God; for it is pleasant; and praise is comely. (Ps. 147:1)

How?

- In God we boast all the day long, and praise thy name for ever. Selah. (Ps. 44:8)

- Make a joyful noise unto the Lord, all ye lands. Serve the Lord with gladness: come before his presence with singing. (Ps. 100:1-2)

- Enter into his gates with thanksgiving, and into his courts with praise: be thankful unto him, and bless his name. (Ps. 100:4)

Sharpening Your Spiritual Tools

- Let my mouth be filled with thy praise and with thy honour all the day. (Ps. 71:8)

- I will bless the Lord at all times: his praise shall continually be in my mouth. (Ps. 34:1)

- From the rising of the sun unto the going down of the same the Lord's name is to be praised. (Ps. 113:3)

- Give unto the Lord the glory due unto his name; worship the Lord in the beauty of holiness. (Ps. 29:2)

- I will praise thee, O Lord my God, with all my heart: and I will glorify thy name for evermore. (Ps. 86:12)

Normally, we associate praise and worship to God when we attend church and participate in the worship service. Even though church assembly is one form of worship, it

Tool #3 – Praise and Worship

should not be the only time we give Him praise. We are not confined to praising God only in a particular setting or location, but every day that we awake to a new dawning is another chance afforded us to give Him glory. For, it is His breath in our lungs that allows us to keep living. He is our Life Giver; He created us to bring honor to Him and to bless His name. So, out of the depth of our soul, the very core of our being, we should joyfully and consistently boast in and celebrate the true and living God, our Maker.

Living a lifestyle of holiness, righteousness, and godliness is worship to God, as this is how God's Word commands us to live. When we fashion our lives in obedience and reverence to Him, God's name is magnified. It brings pleasure unto Him, seeing His children follow in His ways. Humbling ourselves and not conforming to the pattern of this world keeps us aligned with the Spirit of God, allowing Him to lead and guide us in the way of truth. Our hearts shall be one of gratitude and thankfulness unto God; even though, we are oftentimes faced with trials and tests of this life, God promised us that He will be present to help us when we call on Him. He's given victory through His Son, Jesus, unto all who would believe in Him.

Therefore, we shall praise God in how we speak, with words full of mercy, grace, and truth, and we shall bless God with the "fruit of our lips," (Heb. 13:15). We shall praise God in how we hear and what we listen to, making sure we are hearing the way of the Lord. We shall praise Him in how we see, that we set our sights on things above, looking to Jesus, our Redeemer, Lord and Savior. We shall praise Him in how we think — regarding, considering, and believing those things that God's Word teaches us. As we die daily to our flesh, take a back seat, and give God control of our lives, we are worshiping Him in a far greater capacity.

Tool Tips:

Tool #3 – Praise and Worship

- Always honor and give reverence to God; give praise to His holy name.

- Sing songs of praise to God.

- Read and study scriptures that give praise to God.

- Use your talents to praise God, such as singing in a choir, playing an instrument as a musician, and being a praise dancer.

- Make praise and worship a lifelong expression to God.

Application

What do you think is the importance of ***praise and worship?***

_____
_____
_____

Sharpening Your Spiritual Tools

_____

_____

How does this tool improve your daily walk with God?

_____

_____

_____

_____

_____

What are some ways you exhibit praise and worship?

_____

_____

_____

_____

_____

CHAPTER 4

Tool #4 – Communion

Sharpening Your Spiritual Tools

Why?

- And as they were eating, Jesus took bread, and blessed it, and brake it, and gave it to the disciples, and said, "Take, eat; this is my body." And he took the cup, and gave thanks, and gave it to them, saying, "Drink ye all of it; For this is my blood of the new testament, which is shed for many for the remission of sins." (Matt. 26:26-28)

- The cup of blessing, which we bless, is it not the communion of the blood of Christ? The bread which we break, is it not the communion of the body of Christ? (1 Cor. 10:16)

- For the bread of God is he which cometh down from heaven, and giveth life unto the world. (John 6:33)

- And Jesus said unto them, "I am the bread of life: he that cometh to me shall never hunger; and he that believeth on me shall never thirst." (John 6:35)

- I am that bread of life. (John 6:48)

- This is the bread which cometh down from heaven, that a man may eat thereof, and not die. I am the living bread which came down from heaven: if any man eat of this bread, he shall live for ever: and the bread that I give is my flesh, which I will give for the life of the world. (John 6:50-51)

How?

- Then Jesus said unto them, "Verily, verily, I say unto you, Except ye eat the flesh of the Son of man, and drink his blood, ye have no life in you.

> Whoso eateth my flesh, and drinketh my blood, hath eternal life; and I will raise him up at the last day. For my flesh is meat indeed, and my blood is drink indeed. He that eateth my flesh, and drinketh my blood, dwelleth in me, and I in him. As the living Father hath sent me, and I live by the Father: so he that eateth me, even he shall live by me. This is that bread which came down from heaven: not as your fathers did eat manna, and are dead: he that eateth of this bread shall live forever." (John 6:53-58)

- For I have received of the Lord that which also I delivered unto you, that the Lord Jesus the same night in which he was betrayed took bread: And when he had given thanks, he brake it, and said, "Take, eat: this is my body, which is broken for you: this do in remembrance of me." After the same manner also he took

Tool #4 – Communion

the cup, when he had supped, saying, "This cup is the new testament in my blood: this do ye, as oft as ye drink it, in remembrance of me." For as often as ye eat this bread, and drink this cup, ye do shew the Lord's death till he come. Wherefore whosoever shall eat this bread, and drink this cup of the Lord, unworthily, shall be guilty of the body and blood of the Lord. But let a man examine himself, and so let him eat of that bread, and drink of that cup. For he that eateth and drinketh unworthily, eateth and drinketh damnation to himself, not discerning the Lord's body. (1 Cor. 11:23-29)

- And as they did eat, Jesus took bread, and blessed, and brake it, and gave to them, and said, "Take, eat: this is my body." And he took the cup, and when he had given thanks, he gave it to them: and they all drank of it. And

Sharpening Your Spiritual Tools

> he said unto them, "This is my blood of the new testament, which is shed for many." (Mark 14:22-24)

- And he took bread, and gave thanks, and brake it, and gave unto them, saying, "This is my body which is given for you: this do in remembrance of me." Likewise, also the cup after supper, saying, "This cup is the new testament in my blood, which is shed for you." (Luke 22:19-20)

Oh, the love, oh, the joy, and the sweet communion of Almighty God!

God created us to have fellowship with Him—an intimate and personal relationship where we are in constant communication with Him. Even though man's intimacy of fellowship with God was broken because of sin, it was restored through Jesus's sacrifice on the cross. Jesus died so that all who believe in Him can have eternal life and victory. We don't have to live in condemnation,

Tool #4 – Communion

guilt, and shame. Rather, we have life, liberty, and freedom to be who God has called us to be. Now, we can all come boldly before the Father and have our own encounter with Him. Thank you, Lord!

Communion connects us to God. It symbolizes Jesus's body that was broken, and His blood that was shed for us, bringing remembrance to what Jesus accomplished on our behalf, and breaking down the wall of separation that was between us and the Father. We share in Christ's death when we partake of the bread and the cup. The elements we use when taking communion may vary, though crackers and grape juice are normally used. Yet, whatever is used to represent Jesus's body and His blood, ask God's blessings that it become symbols for supernatural signs, wonders, and miracles to take place. It is a heart of thankfulness and gratitude that we express to God for sending His Son to pay the penalty of sin for us, and the benefits we gained as a result.

Even though many churches have specific times they receive communion, it can be taken at any time and any place; however, we should examine ourselves and give reverence to the meaning of why we are doing it. As followers of Christ, are we walking in life paths and in the truth that conforms to Jesus's likeness, since we are God's visible representation on the earth? Are we submitted to the way of Jesus, considering His act of obedience, because of His love for us? Whenever we take communion, we should remember that, because of Jesus's blood that was shed for us, we no longer have to be under the dominion of Satan, but walk in the promises of God, without fear or hesitation.

Oh, the joy, oh, the love, may we know the sweetness to commune with God!

Tool Tips:

- Pray before or after taking communion.

Tool #4 – Communion

- Take communion often. You may use bread/water, or juice/crackers, etc.

- Examine yourself before taking communion.

- Keep in remembrance the victory gained for us through Christ's sacrifice.

- Know the blood of Jesus is powerful to save, heal, set free, and deliver.

Application

What do you think is the importance of ***communion***?

_____
_____
_____
_____
_____

Sharpening Your Spiritual Tools

How does this tool improve your daily walk with God?

_____

_____

_____

_____

_____

How does taking communion benefit you?

_____

_____

_____

_____

_____

_____

CHAPTER 5

Tool #5 – Fasting

Why?

- Then, I proclaimed a fast there, at the river of Ahava, that we might afflict ourselves before our God, to seek of him a right way for us, and for our little ones, and for all our substance. (Ezra 8:21)

- And Jonah began to enter into the city a day's journey, and he cried, and said, "Yet, forty days, and Nineveh shall be overthrown." So, the people of Nineveh believed God, and proclaimed a fast, and put on sackcloth, from the greatest of them even to the least of them. For word came unto the king of Nineveh, and he arose from his throne, and he laid his robe from him, and covered him with sackcloth, and sat in ashes. And he caused it to be proclaimed and published through Nineveh by the decree of the king and his nobles, saying, "Let neither man nor beast, herd nor flock, taste any thing: let them not feed, nor drink water: But let man and beast be covered with sackcloth, and cry mightily unto God: yea, let them turn every one from his evil way, and from the violence that is in their hands. Who can tell if God will turn and repent, and turn away from his fierce anger, that we perish not?" And God saw their works, that they turned from their evil way; and God repented of the evil, that he had said that he would do unto them; and he did it not. (Jon. 3:4-10)

- Lord, have mercy on my son: for he is lunatick, and sore vexed: for ofttimes he falleth into the fire, and oft into the water. And I brought him to thy disciples, and they could not cure him. Then Jesus answered and said, "O faithless and perverse generation, how long shall I be with you? how long shall I suffer you? bring him hither to me." And Jesus rebuked the devil; and he departed out of him: and the child was cured from that very hour. Then came the disciples to Jesus apart, and said, "Why could not we cast him out?" And Jesus said unto them, "Because of your unbelief: for verily I say unto you, If ye have faith as a grain of mustard seed, ye shall say unto this mountain, 'Remove hence to yonder place;' and it shall remove; and nothing shall be impossible unto you. Howbeit this kind goeth not out but by prayer and fasting." (Matt. 17:15-21)

- And Cornelius said, "Four days ago I was fasting until this hour;

and at the ninth hour I prayed in my house, and behold, a man stood before me in bright clothing. And said, 'Cornelius, thy prayer is heard, and thine alms are had in remembrance in the sight of God.'" (Acts 10:30–31)

How?

- And she was a widow of about fourscore and four years, which departed not from the temple, but served God with fastings and prayers night and day. (Luke 2:37)

- Go, gather together all the Jews that are present in Shushan, and fast ye for me, and neither eat nor drink three days, night or day; I also and my maidens will fast likewise; and so will I go in unto the king, which is not according to the law: and if I perish, I perish. (Esther 4:16)

- And I set my face unto the Lord God, to seek by prayer and supplications, with fasting, and sackcloth, and ashes. (Dan. 9:3)

- And Jehoshaphat feared, and set himself to seek the Lord, and proclaimed a fast throughout all Judah. (2 Chron. 20:3)

- And it came to pass, when I heard these words, that I sat down and wept, and mourned certain days, and fasted, and prayed before the God of heaven. (Neh. 1:4)

- David therefore besought God for the child; and David fasted, and went in, and lay all night upon the earth. (2 Sam. 12:16)

Tool #5 – Fasting

- Sanctify ye a fast, call a solemn assembly, gather the elders and all the inhabitants of the land into the house of the Lord your God, and cry unto the Lord. (Joel 1:14)

- "Therefore, also now," saith the Lord, "turn ye even to me with all your heart, and with fasting, and with weeping, and with mourning: And rend your heart, and not your garments, and turn unto the Lord your God: for he is gracious and merciful, slow to anger, and of great kindness, and repenteth him of the evil." (Joel 2:12-13)

- Then, all the children of Israel, and all the people, went up, and came unto the house of God, and wept, and sat there before the Lord, and fasted that day until even, and offered burnt offerings and peace offerings before the Lord. (Judg. 20:26)

- Moreover when ye fast, be not, as the hypocrites, of a sad countenance: for they disfigure their faces, that they may appear unto men to fast. Verily, I say unto you, They have their reward. But thou, when thou fastest, anoint thine head, and wash thy face. (Matt. 6:16-17)

Whether we are seeking God's guidance and direction, wanting to draw closer to God, need healing for our body, or simply need God to move on our behalf, fasting is a way to gain victory in our lives. It is more than turning down a plate of food; it is a humbling experience that allows us to exercise discipline over our fleshly nature and our carnal way of thinking. This helps to strip us of selfish appetites, desires, passions, and pleasures that are not in line with the will of God. Throughout Scripture, it is noted how fasting helped those dealing with difficult situations to overcome the works of the Enemy. Fasting is a time of consecration, where we take the focus off ourselves and devote more time pursuing God and His more excellent way. In our submission, our spiritual senses are sharpened; we obtain insight, and we are made stronger as we draw power from God.

Fasting is even more powerful and effective when combined with prayer and meditation on God's Word. They enhance each other, giving us life and nourishing our soul. While our bodies may weaken when we refrain from natural food, we can trust God to sustain us and be our strength. Since we seek Him in a time of supplication, intercession, and thanksgiving, we are able to feed on His Word, positioning ourselves to spiritually increase. We should allow the "Holy Spirit of Truth" to lead and aid us in times of fasting, so that growth, change, and transformation will take place in and through us.

While many believers refrain from fasting as part of the Christian walk and journey, it should be the opposite. Fasting should be viewed as necessary, and as a normal part of the believer's lifestyle. We should not think about what we're giving up, but think of the fruit it shall yield as it revives, restores, and refreshes us. Fasting is not intended to harm us, but to help us become a more disciplined believer; the end result is to be more alive to God — glorifying, magnifying, and bringing honor to His name!

Tool Tips:

- Seek God during times of fasting.

- Combine fasting with prayer.

- Read and meditate on God's Word while fasting.

Tool #5 – Fasting

- Honor your commitment to fast, as this will help discipline you.

- Journal any new revelation you receive from God.

Application

What do you think is the importance of ***fasting***?

_____
_____
_____
_____
_____

How does this tool improve your daily walk with God?

_____
_____
_____

Sharpening Your Spiritual Tools

_____

_____

How does fasting benefit you?

_____

_____

_____

_____

_____

CHAPTER 6

Tool #6 – Hearing from God

Why?

- But he said, "Yea rather, blessed are they that hear the word of God, and keep it." (Luke 11:28)

- Out of heaven he made thee to hear his voice, that he might instruct thee: and upon earth he shewed thee his great fire; and thou heardest his words out of the midst of the fire. (Deut. 4:36)

- Observe and hear all these words which I command thee, that it may go well with thee, and with thy children after thee for ever, when thou doest that which is good and right in the sight of the Lord thy God. (Deut. 12:28)

- Cause me to hear thy lovingkindness in the morning; for in thee do I trust: cause me to know the way

Tool #6 – Hearing from God

wherein I should walk; for I lift up my soul unto thee. (Ps. 143:8)

- My son, hear the instruction of thy father, and forsake not the law of thy mother. (Prov. 1:8)

- Hear, O my son, and receive my sayings; and the years of thy life shall be many. (Prov. 4:10)

- Blessed is the man that heareth me, watching daily at my gates, waiting at the posts of my doors. (Prov. 8:34)

- The ear that heareth the reproof of life abideth among the wise. He that refuseth instruction despiseth his own soul: but he that heareth reproof getteth understanding. (Prov. 15:31-32)

- Hear counsel, and receive instruction, that thou mayest be wise in thy latter end. (Prov. 19:20)

How?

- So then faith cometh by hearing, and hearing by the word of God. (Rom. 10:17)

- Hear instruction, and be wise, and refuse it not. (Prov. 8:33)

- While he yet spake, behold, a bright cloud overshadowed them: and behold a voice out of the cloud, which said, "This is my beloved Son, in whom I am well pleased; hear ye him." (Matt. 17:5)

- Take heed therefore how ye hear: for whosoever hath, to him shall be given; and whosoever hath not, from him shall be taken even

Tool #6 – Hearing from God

that which he seemeth to have. (Luke 8:18)

- My sheep hear my voice, and I know them, and they follow me. (John 10:27)

- Whilst it is said, "Today if ye will hear his voice, harden not your hearts, as in the provocation." (Heb. 3:15)

- Wherefore, my beloved brethren, let every man be swift to hear, slow to speak, slow to wrath. (James 1:19)

- Behold, I stand at the door, and knock: if any man hear my voice, and open the door, I will come in to him, and will sup with him, and he with me. (Rev. 3:20)

Sharpening Your Spiritual Tools

- He that hath ears to hear, let him hear. (Matt. 11:15)

We are often surrounded by many voices —family, friends, coworkers, social media, world views/opinions, and more — but through all the noise, hearing the voice of God is most important. For, we need His wisdom, knowledge, understanding, revelation, and discernment, to help us overcome the circumstances of life. It is the counsel of God that leads, directs, and instructs us in living just and upright, which is pleasing unto Him. However, we must be tuned into His frequency to receive from Him, and to heed His message.

We must quiet ourselves, remove distractions, and spend time listening to the voice of God. God can speak through His Word, a gentle, soft, whispering voice, His audible voice, and through other people. When we need an answer, clarity, or confirmation on an issue, let us seek God's guidance and wait patiently to hear from Him.

Tool #6 – Hearing from God

Sometimes, we hear the answer right away, or it may come later. When hearing from God, we should have peace about what to do, and it should be our guide to give us a favorable outcome.

We were designed to have constant communication and fellowship with the Father. On a daily basis, we should be desirous, in expectation, and in pursuit of hearing His direction for our lives, that He will establish our plans and purposes in righteousness and in truth. When we hear and obey the voice of God, we increase in understanding and are made better, stronger, and wiser. He will lead us through and around the pitfalls, snares, and traps of life. What we hear from God is the truth, and as we follow that in which we hear, we are blessed in return.

Tool Tips:

- Remove distractions and quiet yourself before God.

Sharpening Your Spiritual Tools

- Seek and desire to hear God's voice.

- Listen for His guidance and instructions.

- Let the peace of God in your heart guide you.

- Write down what you are hearing from God.

Application

What do you think is the importance of ***hearing*** from God?

_____
_____
_____
_____
_____

Tool #6 – Hearing from God

How does this tool improve your daily walk with God?

_____
_____
_____
_____
_____

How does God speak to you? Explain.

_____
_____
_____
_____
_____
_____

CHAPTER 7

Tool #7 – Spiritual Sight and Vision

Why?

- Blessed are the pure in heart: for they shall see God. (Matt. 5:8)

- Be sober, be vigilant; because your adversary the devil, as a roaring lion, walketh about, seeking whom he may devour. (1 Pet. 5:8)

- Be not wise in thine own eyes: fear the Lord, and depart from evil. (Prov. 3:7)

- Where there is no vision, the people perish… (Prov. 29:18)

- Open thou mine eyes, that I may behold wondrous things out of thy law. (Ps. 119:18)

- Watch and pray, that ye enter not into temptation: the spirit indeed

Tool #7 – Spiritual Sight and Vision

is willing, but the flesh is weak. (Matt. 26:41)

- Watch therefore, for ye know neither the day nor the hour wherein the Son of man cometh. (Matt. 25:13)

- While we look not at the things which are seen, but at the things which are not seen: for the things which are seen are temporal; but the things which are not seen are eternal. (2 Cor. 4:18)

- The eyes of your understanding being enlightened; that ye may know what is the hope of his calling, and what the riches of the glory of his inheritance in the saints. (Eph. 1:18)

How?

- For we walk by faith, not by sight. (2 Cor. 5:7)

- Looking unto Jesus the author and finisher of our faith… (Heb. 12:2)

- See then that ye walk circumspectly, not as fools, but as wise. (Eph. 5:15)

- Looking for that blessed hope, and the glorious appearing of the great God and our Saviour Jesus Christ. (Titus 2:13)

- Therefore let us not sleep, as do others; but let us watch and be sober. (1 Thess. 5:6)

- Thy word is a lamp unto my feet, and a light unto my path. (Ps. 119:105)

Tool #7 – Spiritual Sight and Vision

- I press toward the mark for the prize of the high calling of God in Christ Jesus. (Phil. 3:14)

- Let thine eyes look right on, and let thine eyelids look straight before thee. (Prov. 4:25)

- If ye then be risen with Christ, seek those things which are above, where Christ sitteth on the right hand of God. Set your affection on things above, not on things on the earth. (Col. 3:1-2)

What we allow to enter through our eye gate is important for us to stay focused and attentive, and remain unhindered as Christians. *How* we see has a direct impact on us, just like *what* we see. We don't merely see with our physical eyes, but also with our spiritual eyes, for we need spiritual vision and insight to see into the realm of the spirit. Our natural

Sharpening Your Spiritual Tools

eyes see what's in front of us, but our spiritual eyes go much deeper than that. Through discernment, revelation, knowledge, and understanding of God's Word, we're able to see light through the darkness, good through the bad, peace through confusion, what's possible through impossibilities, and so on. For we believe in the promises of God, and we look for them to manifest in our lives. Our sights should be set upon Jesus — walking in His ways and observing, considering, and regarding His teachings on a daily basis. We have been called out of the darkness of Satan's bondage and into the light of the gospel of Jesus Christ.

We must be watchful, alert, and of a sound mind, exercising self-restraint and discipline, so we don't become intoxicated with the world views that oppose God's ways and thoughts. It is His way that will lighten our path through holiness and godliness. As we stay fully committed to God, allowing His Holy Spirit to lead

Tool #7 – Spiritual Sight and Vision

us, we will become more aware, sensitive, sharp, and clear in our perception of spiritual recognition.

Our faith in God shall lead us as we strive to go higher in Him. Our trust, confidence, and assurance in the promises of God will keep us as we keep our eyes on Jesus, and the prize that is set before us. We must examine ourselves in line with God's standard, and carefully look to respect His Word as the final authority in our lives. All things we see are now temporary, but the things we don't yet see are eternal.

Tool Tips:

- Pray and seek God for wisdom and the ability to see through the eyes of God.

- Walk in faith of God's Word and believe His Word as the absolute standard.

- Be led by the Holy Spirit of God.

- Seek God's guidance and instruction.

- Set your sight on things above and be Heaven-minded.

Application

What do you think is the importance of having ***spiritual sight and vision***?

_____
_____
_____
_____
_____

How can you use this tool to improve your walk with God?

_____
_____

Tool #7 – Spiritual Sight and Vision

_____
_____
_____

What scriptures speak to you on spiritual sight and vision?

_____
_____
_____
_____
_____

CHAPTER 8

Tool #8 – Confess and Speak God's Word

Why?

- A man shall be satisfied with good by the fruit of his mouth ... (Prov. 12:14)

- A man hath joy by the answer of his mouth: and a word spoken in due season, how good is it! (Prov. 15:23)

- A man's belly shall be satisfied with the fruit of his mouth; and with the increase of his lips shall he be filled. Death and life are in the power of the tongue: and they that love it shall eat the fruit thereof. (Prov. 18:20-21)

- But I say unto you, That every idle word that men shall speak, they shall give account thereof in the day of judgement. For by thy words thou shalt be justified, and

Tool #8 – Confess and Speak God's Word

by thy words thou shall be condemned. (Matt. 12:36-37)

- For verily I say unto you, That whosoever shall say unto this mountain, be thou removed, and be thou cast into the sea; and shall not doubt in his heart, but shall believe that those things which he saith shall come to pass; he shall have whatsoever he saith. (Mark 11:23)

- For he that will love life, and see good days, let him refrain his tongue from evil, and his lips that they speak no guile. (1 Pet. 3:10)

- Talk no more so exceeding proudly; let not arrogancy come out of your mouth: for the Lord is a God of knowledge, and by him actions are weighed. (1 Sam. 2:3)

- Let them shout for joy, and be glad, that favor my righteous cause: yea, let them say continually, Let the Lord be magnified, which hath pleasure in the prosperity of his servant. (Ps. 35:27)

- My tongue shall speak of thy word: for all thy commandments are righteousness. (Ps. 119:172)

- Bless the Lord, ye his angels, that excel in strength, that do his commandments, hearkening unto the voice of his word. (Ps. 103:20)

How?

- I will declare thy name unto my brethren: in the midst of the congregation will I praise thee. (Ps. 22:22)

Tool #8 – Confess and Speak God's Word

- I shall not die, but live, and declare the works of the Lord. (Ps. 118:17)

- Thou shalt also decree a thing, and it shall be established unto thee: and the light shall shine upon thy ways. (Job 22:28)

- I will bless the Lord at all times: his praise shall continually be in my mouth. (Ps. 34:1)

- Let my mouth be filled with thy praise and with thy honour all the day. (Ps. 71:8)

- As it is written, I have made thee a father of many nations, before him whom he believed, even God, who quickeneth the dead, and calleth those things which be not as though they were. (Rom. 4:17)

Sharpening Your Spiritual Tools

- And my tongue shall speak of thy righteousness and of thy praise all the day long. (Ps. 35:28)

- Let the redeemed of the Lord say so, whom he hath redeemed from the hand of the enemy. (Ps. 107:2)

- I will speak of the glorious honour of thy majesty, and of thy wondrous works. (Ps. 145:5)

Confessing God's Word is powerful. It gives us life, health, strength, encouragement, joy, peace, comfort, and so much more! What we confess, speak, declare, and decree determines the fruit that will be produced in our lives. Our mouth has power with which we can bless or curse, speak life or death, and change and shift the atmosphere of our situations and circumstances. Daily, we can speak boldly, and with confidence, for Jesus gave us power over the Enemy. When we align

Tool #8 – Confess and Speak God's Word

our faith with God's will, we can have His promises come to pass in our lives. As we speak what we hear God say unto us, His goodness surrounds us, for even the angels of God obey and give heed to the sound of His Word; we know that God's Word does not return empty, but does what it is purposed to do.

We must guard our mouth and speak words that build up and not tear down — words that are wholesome and gracious, and not evil and corrupt. Let our speech be pleasing to God's ears. We can't be arrogant and boastful with our words, but we must speak the wisdom of God, declaring light in dark situations and life in dead situations. We cannot be moved by what we see or feel, but shall have faith in God. We're made in God's image and likeness. Just as God spoke the earth into existence by His words, our faith-filled words can cause that which is not, into existence. We exercise authority on the earth, communicating and establishing God's will and desires. Even so, we shall daily offer God praise, honor, and glory, speaking blessings unto His name, declaring His greatness in the heavens and on the earth.

As we come into agreement and declare what God says, know that change is coming unto us. God honors His Word! He is able to rearrange, reposition, realign, and shift whatever is necessary to bring us to a place of power, victory, and restoration in Him.

Tool Tips:

- Read and meditate on God's Word consistently.

- Speak and confess God's Word daily.

- Make declarations of faith in agreement with God's Word.

Tool #8 – Confess and Speak God's Word

- Speak words of victory, knowing our words have power and authority.

- Don't confess words of doubt, fear, and unbelief.

Application

What do you think is the importance of ***confessing and speaking*** God's Word?

_____

_____

_____

_____

_____

How can you use this tool to improve your walk with God?

_____

_____

Sharpening Your Spiritual Tools

_____

_____

_____

Do you have daily confessions? If so, what are they?

_____

_____

_____

_____

_____

Prayer for Salvation

Almighty God, thank You for sending Your Son, Jesus, to die for my sins. I believe Jesus died and You raised Him from the dead for my justification. I repent of my sin and turn from my own ways. I turn to You to be Lord and Savior over my life. I commit my life to You. I thank You, Lord, for saving me, and giving me new and eternal life through Jesus Christ. In Jesus's name. Amen!

Romans 3:23 – "For all have sinned, and come short of the glory of God."

Romans 6:23 – "For the wages of sin is death, but the gift of God is eternal life through Jesus Christ our Lord."

Sharpening Your Spiritual Tools

Romans 10:9-10 – "That if thou shalt confess with thy mouth the Lord Jesus, and shalt believe in thine heart that God hath raised him from the dead, thou shalt be saved. For with the heart man believeth unto righteousness; and with the mouth confession is made unto salvation."

AFTERWORD

God is Alpha and Omega, the beginning and the end, the first and the last. His kingdom is an everlasting kingdom and rules over all. He is our Creator and knows what is best for us. We were created for His glory (Isa. 43:7). Allow Him to hit the refresh button in your life, where He is able to make that which is bad, good, that which is good, great, and that which is great, excellent. Let every day be a day of thanksgiving and gratitude to the Lord, as He allows and sustains us to see a new day of His mercy, grace, and loving kindness. We should never cease to trust, believe, and acknowledge Him, concerning our pathway of life, but let us strive to go in the way of the Lord for the rest of our days, joining in His way of seeing, hearing, speaking, thinking, being, and doing. For, it is through Him that our greatness resides. God's way is perfect (Ps. 18:30), and it is in Him that we live, move, and have our being (Acts 17:28). May we always be abounding and going higher in God, knowing growth will take place, for it's bound to happen!

CPSIA information can be obtained
at www.ICGtesting.com
Printed in the USA
BVHW051939200423
662743BV00012B/214